Cambridge **Discovery Education**™

▶ INTERACTIVE READERS

Series editor: Bob Hastings

LOST
THE MYSTERY OF
AMELIA EARHART

A1+

Kenna Bourke

CAMBRIDGE UNIVERSITY PRESS
Cambridge, New York, Melbourne, Madrid, Cape Town,
Singapore, São Paulo, Delhi, Mexico City

Cambridge University Press
32 Avenue of the Americas, New York, NY 10013-2473, USA

www.cambridge.org
Information on this title: www.cambridge.org/9781107693357

First published 2014
Reprinted 2014

Printed in Hong Kong, China, by Golden Cup Printing Company Limited

A catalog record for this publication is available from the British Library.

Library of Congress Cataloging-in-Publication Data

Bourke, Kenna.
  Lost: the mystery of Amelia Earhart / Kenna Bourke.
    pages cm. -- (Cambridge discovery interactive readers)
  ISBN 978-1-107-69335-7 (pbk. : alk. paper)
  1. Earhart, Amelia, 1897-1937--Juvenile literature. 2. Women air pilots--United States--
Biography--Juvenile literature. 3. English language--Textbooks for foreign speakers. 4. Readers
(Elementary) I. Title.

TL540.E3B63 2013
629.13092--dc23

                              2013025120

ISBN 978-1-107-69335-7

Additional resources for this publication at www.cambridge.org

Cambridge University Press has no responsibility for the persistence or
accuracy of URLs for external or third-party Internet Web sites referred to in
this publication and does not guarantee that any content on such Web sites is,
or will remain, accurate or appropriate.

Layout services, art direction, book design, and photo research: Q2ABillSMITH GROUP
Editorial services: Hyphen S.A.
Audio production: CityVox, New York
Video production: Q2ABillSMITH GROUP

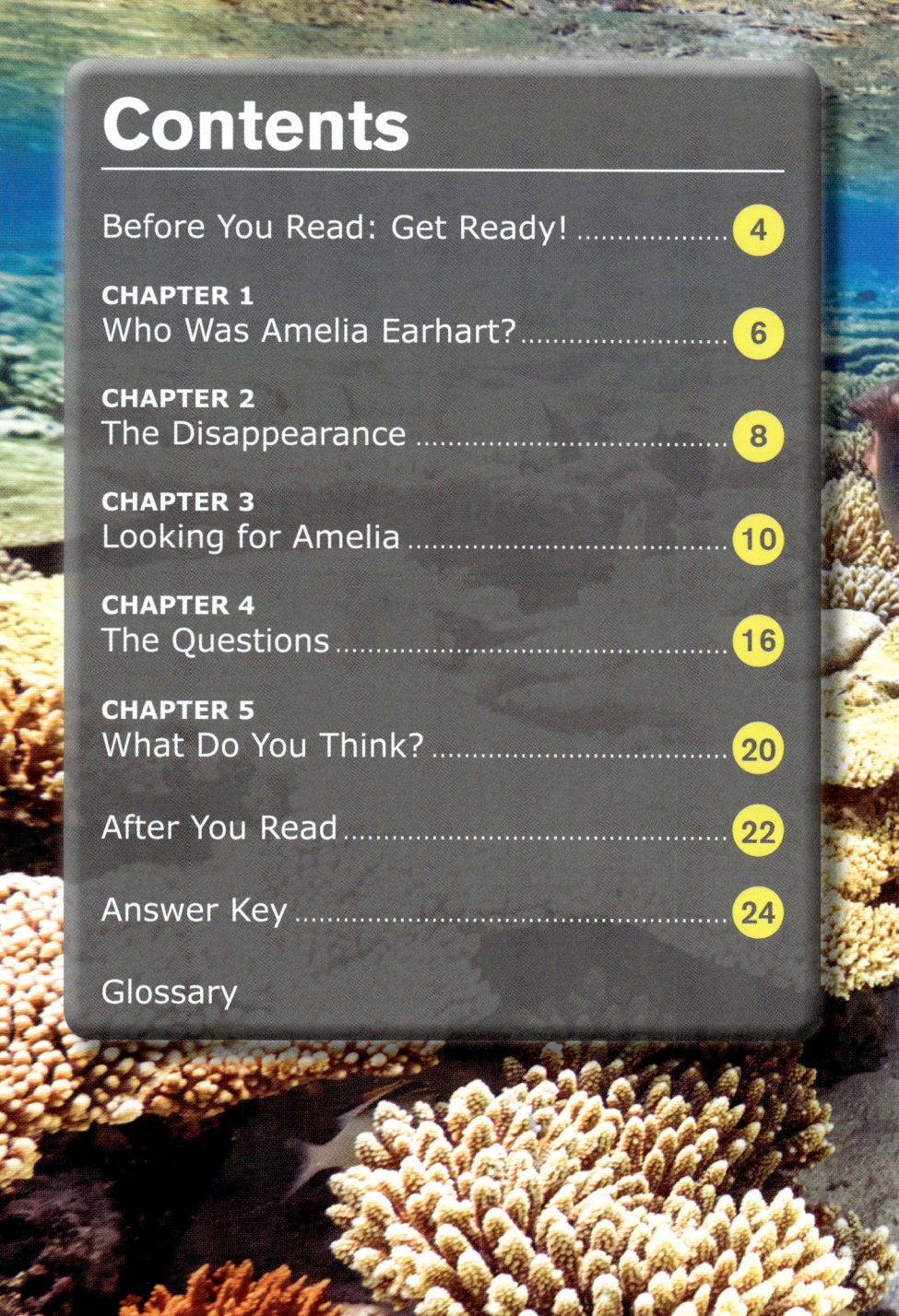

Contents

Before You Read:
Get Ready!

Words to Know

Look at the pictures. Then complete the sentences below with the correct words.

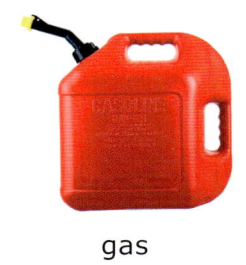
gas

island

land

ocean

ship

take off

1 A plane needs _____ to fly.

2 When planes go up, they _____ .

3 The Pacific is the biggest _____ in the world.

4 Look! The plane is going to _____ . It's almost here!

5 Let's swim out to the beautiful _____ .

6 A _____ can carry many people on the water.

Words to Know

Read the paragraphs. Then complete the sentences below with the correct highlighted words.

It is June of 1937. Amelia Earhart and Fred Noonan are trying to fly around the world. The first part of their flight is to Lae, New Guinea. They are only 11,000 kilometers from home, but now they have to cross the Pacific Ocean. They need to stop at a small island, called Howland Island, to get more gas. But Amelia and Fred never get to Howland Island. And nobody ever sees them again.

People looked for Amelia and Fred. Even today, they're still looking. What happened on the last flight? Did the plane fall out of the sky into the ocean? Did Amelia get hurt? Did Fred break a bone? Were they dead, or were they alive on another island?

1 He has to go to the airport quickly. His _____ leaves one hour from now.

2 Ouch! My new shoes are too small. They _____ my feet when I walk in them.

3 The longest _____ in a person's body is in the leg.

4 Don't stand on that old chair! You can _____ off!

5 My grandmother is alive, but my grandfather is _____.
He died in 2005.

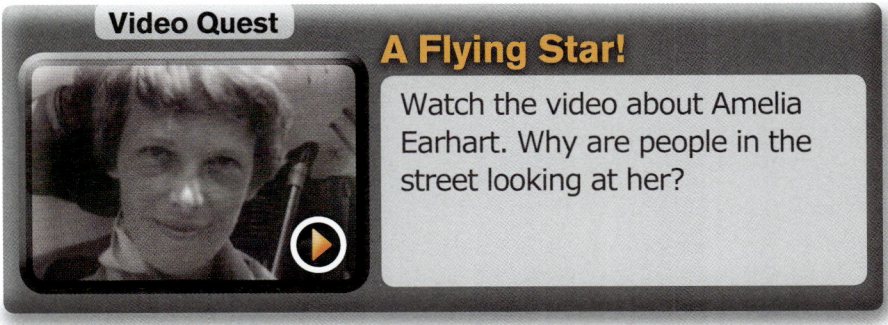

Video Quest

A Flying Star!

Watch the video about Amelia Earhart. Why are people in the street looking at her?

Amelia Earhart was big news!

CHAPTER 1

Who Was Amelia Earhart?

AT FIRST, THERE WERE VERY FEW PLANES AND VERY FEW PEOPLE TO FLY THEM.

Airplanes and flying were very new things in the early 1900s. There weren't many pilots (people who fly planes), and there were even fewer women pilots! Then one day, Amelia Earhart came along: a woman *and* a pilot!

In December 1920, Amelia goes for her first ride in a plane. After that ride she knows that she wants to fly planes, so she takes lessons. In 1932, she flies across the Atlantic Ocean – alone!

The whole world knows about Amelia Earhart now. A newspaper calls Amelia "Queen of the Air." She is famous. Everywhere she goes, people come to see her. They take pictures.

By 1937, Amelia Earhart is a very good pilot, and she's ready to fly around the world. She wants to be the first woman to do this.

Amelia knows she can't do it alone, so she chooses Fred Noonan to go with her. Fred's a navigator. The navigator's main job is reading the map and choosing the best way to go. Fred and Amelia need a good plane to fly around the world in. They choose a Lockheed *Electra*.

On June 1, 1937, Amelia and Fred take off from Florida, USA. The journey is 29,000 miles (47,000 kilometers) . . . but can they do it? The world is watching!

Amelia Earhart and Fred Noonan

CHAPTER 2

The Disappearance

SOMEWHERE OVER THE PACIFIC OCEAN, JULY 2, 1937 . . .

Fred is trying to find Howland Island. There's a ship called the _Itasca_ near the island. It's waiting to help them. Fred uses the sun and a map to look for Howland. But the island is very small. Maybe it's there below them, but Fred and Amelia can't find it.

They fly around, looking for Howland. Amelia is talking to the ship, but then the radio stops working. Why? People in Lae thought they saw smoke coming from the radio antenna before Amelia took off. Did the radio break? What can they do?

A radio antenna

Some people think they were in the wrong place, 640 kilometers away, near Nikumaroro Island. Did they go there because it was the only other place they could land their plane?

When the tide[1] is high, the water around Nikumaroro is **deep**. There's nowhere to land a plane. So maybe when the *Electra* had no more gas, it fell into the **ocean** and Amelia and Fred died.

But when the tide is low, you can see a coral reef on Nikumaroro Island. You can land a plane there! So maybe the *Electra* landed on the island.

If Amelia and Fred got to Nikumaroro, they probably died quickly. It's very hot there, and there's no clean water to drink.

But maybe they found food and water and lived on Nikumaroro for some time.

[1]**tide:** when the ocean goes up and down twice a day

A coral reef

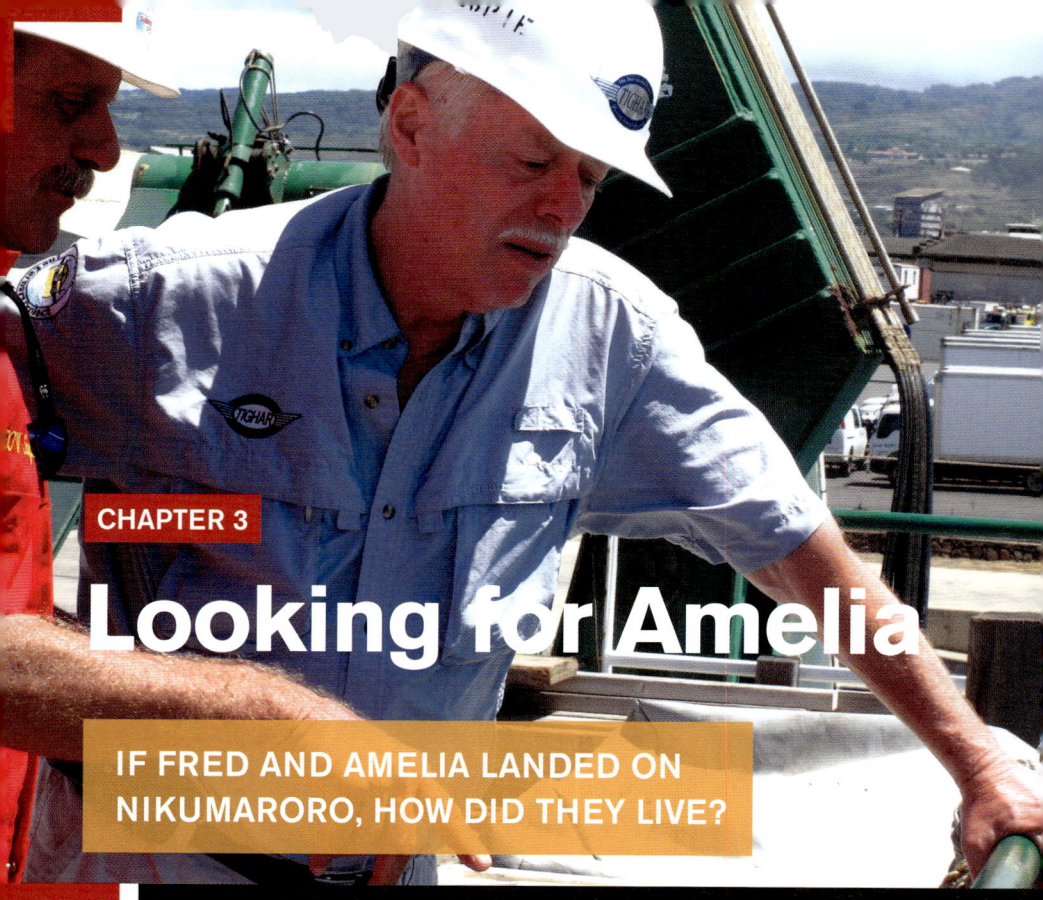

CHAPTER 3

Looking for Amelia

IF FRED AND AMELIA LANDED ON NIKUMARORO, HOW DID THEY LIVE?

In late 1938, some British people begin to live on Nikumaroro. Gerald Gallagher is one of them. He finds some important **evidence**. He thinks the *Electra* landed on the island, but in 1941, he dies.

Fifty years later, in 1991, Ric Gillespie thinks Gallagher was right. He and his **team** start looking for Amelia on Nikumaroro. They also find some important evidence.

Fire and Bones

1940 Gallagher finds old **fires** and the bones of a woman about 1.67-1.79 meters tall. That's how tall Amelia was!

1997 Gillespie's team sees old fires. Someone cooked food! And big **shells**. They're upside down so they catch rainwater.

2010 The team finds fish and bird bones. Someone ate here! Then they find an old finger bone. Is it Amelia's?

Bottles

1940 Gallagher finds a bottle near the woman's bones. It's empty. Maybe Fred and Amelia used it for rainwater.

2010 The team finds **pieces** of glass and many bottles. The bottoms of some bottles are black from fire. Did Amelia and Fred boil[2] water to make it safe to drink?

....

[2]**boil:** make something like water or milk very, very hot

Possible evidence of Amelia on Nikumaroro, including aircraft skin and shoe heels

?

ANALYZE

What things can people use to catch rainwater?

Makeup and a knife

2010 There's a bottle of 1930s **makeup**. Maybe it's *Dr. Berry's Freckle Cream*! Amelia had freckles,[3] but she didn't like them. She didn't want people to see them, so she put makeup on her freckles.

The bottle is important. It's in five pieces. The team finds four pieces in one place, but the fifth piece is a few meters away. It's near some turtle bones. There are also parts of a knife. It's like the knife Amelia had. Did Amelia and Fred eat turtles? Did they use the glass and the knife to cut food?

[3]**freckles:** small brown circles on a person's face

A turtle

A coconut crab

Shoes

1940 Gallagher finds an American-made woman's shoe under a tree.

1991 A coconut crab runs by. Near the crab, there's part of a black shoe. It's an American-made woman's shoe from the 1930s! The team finds a piece of a man's shoe, too. Are these Fred and Amelia's shoes?

People took pictures of Amelia in Indonesia a few days before her last flight. In the photos, she's wearing black shoes like the ones they found on the island.

Radio messages

July 2, 1937, 7:42 a.m.

Amelia and Fred are in the *Electra*. They're going to Howland Island . . . they think. The people on the *Itasca* are talking to Amelia on the radio. Amelia says there's a problem. The plane needs gas.

"We must be on you, but cannot see you – but gas is running low," says Amelia. "We are flying at 1,000 feet."

1,000 feet? That's only 300 meters! Something bad is happening. The plane is too low.

At 9:00 a.m., the people on the ship can't hear Amelia anymore. There's no noise from the radio.

July 2 – July 18, 1937

People in the United States, Canada, Hawaii, and Australia say they hear radio messages from Amelia's plane. So Amelia must be somewhere. She can't be dead if she's sending messages!

One of the people, Mabel Larremore, from Texas, USA, says Amelia and Fred are on a small island. They're both hurt. The plane is partly on land, partly in the water.

There are 120 more radio messages from Amelia. But then the messages stop. Where is she? Where is the *Electra*? Ships look for them but don't find anything. By July 19, everyone thinks Amelia Earhart and Fred Noonan are dead.

Video Quest

Radio Messages

Watch the video about someone hearing a message from Amelia. What does she hear?

CHAPTER 4

The Questions

BUT THERE ARE SOME QUESTIONS TO ANSWER.

Where's the plane?

Ric Gillespie thinks Amelia's plane landed on Nikumaroro, but where is it? A ship, the *Norwich City*, sank[4] there in 1929. You could see it under the sea for 70 years. So why can't we see Amelia's plane?

There are pieces of something on and near the island. But are they pieces of an airplane? And are they pieces of *Amelia's* airplane?

Gillespie thinks so. But people lived on Nikumaroro before Gillespie started to look for Amelia there. Maybe the pieces Gillespie found are from something they used.

[4]**sink:** go under the water

Where are Amelia and Fred's bodies?

Gallagher found bones about the right **size** for a woman like Amelia. Gillespie talked to people who lived on Nikumaroro many years ago. They also say that a woman's bones were there. But where are those bones now? Nobody knows.

Gillespie found a finger bone. Scientists[5] looked at the bone, but they can't say it's Amelia's. Some people say it's from a turtle!

And what about Fred's body and bones? What happened to them?

Gillespie thinks that after Amelia and Fred died, coconut crabs ate the bodies. Coconut crabs are big, and they eat dead animals, so it's possible.

[5]**scientist:** a person who studies things like plants and animals

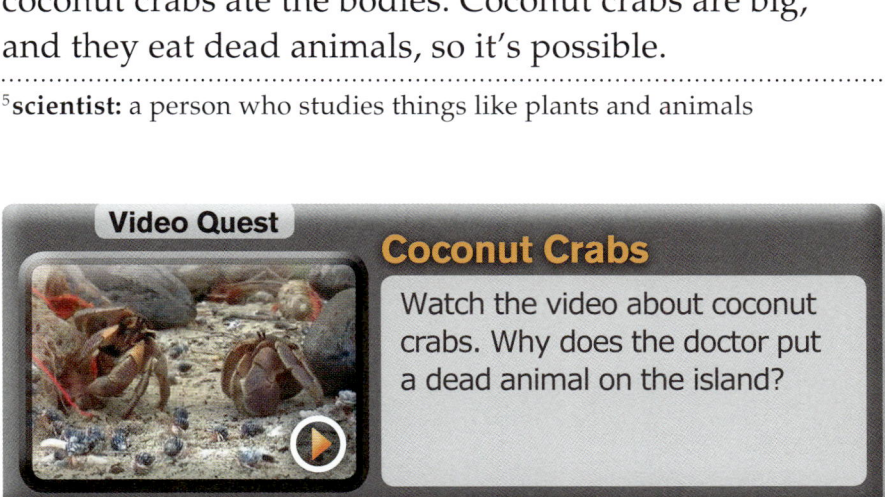

Video Quest

Coconut Crabs

Watch the video about coconut crabs. Why does the doctor put a dead animal on the island?

How about the shoes and makeup?

The pieces of the shoe on Nikumaroro come from a woman's shoe, but they were from a big shoe. Maybe too big for Amelia. Some people say that Amelia had small feet. But nobody knows Amelia's shoe size.

Nobody lived on Nikumaroro until 1938. That year, some British people and people from the Gilbert Islands went there. But by 1965, there was nobody. Life on the island was too hard.

Did other American women go to the island in the 1930s? Maybe the shoe is theirs and not Amelia's. What about the makeup? Maybe someone left that there, too.

The beach at Nikumaroro Island

Were the radio messages real?

Amelia sent radio messages, but did she send 120 messages? Probably not.

Some people like to make up[6] things, especially when something bad happens. In 1937, a few people sent radio messages and said they were from Amelia, but they weren't. Many people didn't believe any of the messages was true.

Ric Gillespie's team read all 120 radio messages again. They think 57 of them were really from Amelia. They think that after Amelia and Fred landed on Nikumaroro, they started the plane's **engine** to send messages. They sent messages this way for a few days before the plane fell off the reef into the deep water.

....

[6]**make up:** say things that aren't true

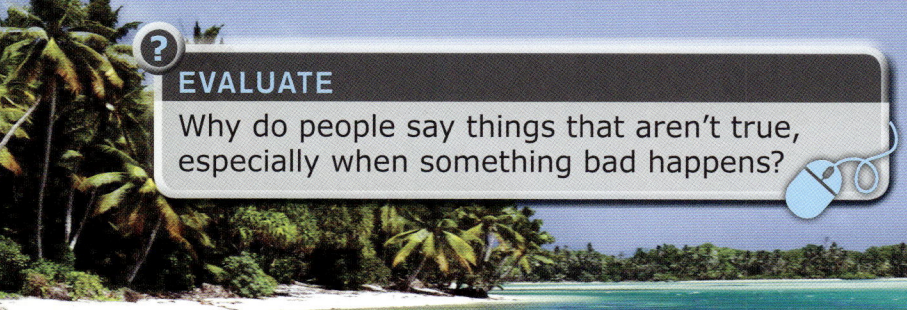

?

EVALUATE

Why do people say things that aren't true, especially when something bad happens?

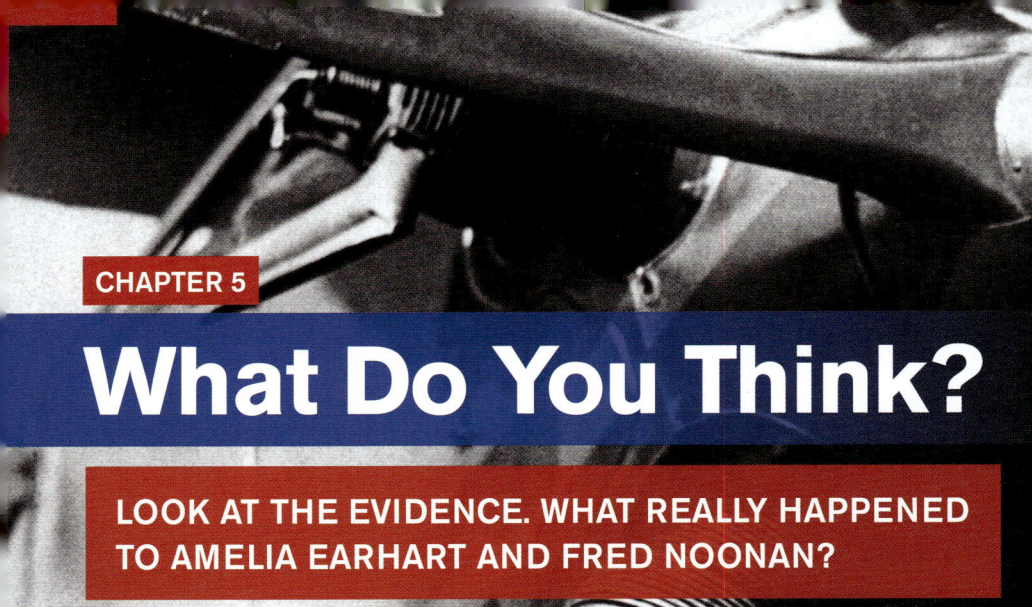

CHAPTER 5

What Do You Think?

LOOK AT THE EVIDENCE. WHAT REALLY HAPPENED TO AMELIA EARHART AND FRED NOONAN?

Evidence	They lived on the island	They died in the ocean
The plane	It landed on the reef and then fell into the sea.	It crashed into the ocean.
Bottles, makeup, knife	They're from the 1930s. Nobody lived on the island until 1938.	People visited the island and left them there.
Shoes	One is an American-made woman's shoe. It's black. Amelia wore shoes like this.	The shoe is bigger than Amelia's feet.
Radio messages	Many people around the world heard messages. The plane had to be on land to send messages.	We know people made up some of the messages, maybe all of them.

Evidence	They lived on the island	They died in the ocean
Bones	Gallagher found bones about Amelia's size. Gillespie found a finger bone.	Where are Amelia's other bones? We don't know it's a human finger bone. Maybe it's a turtle bone. Nobody found Fred's bones.
The bodies	After Amelia and Fred died, crabs ate the bodies and took away the bones.	Amelia and Fred died in the ocean.

Do you think we are ever going to find out what really happened to Amelia Earhart?

After You Read

Read the sentences and choose (A) (True) or (B) (False).

1 Amelia and Fred didn't land in Lae.
   (A) True
   (B) False

2 Fred's job was reading the map and choosing how to get to places.
   (A) True
   (B) False

3 Amelia and Fred wanted to go to Nikumaroro, then Howland Island.
   (A) True
   (B) False

4 Gallagher found bones, bottles, and a shoe on the island.
   (A) True
   (B) False

5 Gillespie and his team started looking for Amelia and Fred on Howland Island.
   (A) True
   (B) False

6 It's possible Fred and Amelia ate fish and birds on Nikumaroro.
   (A) True
   (B) False

7 Nobody knows where Fred's body and bones are.
   (A) True
   (B) False

8 Everybody thinks Amelia's plane fell from the sky into the ocean.
   (A) True
   (B) False

Read the sentences and choose Ⓐ, Ⓑ, or Ⓒ.

1 Nikumaroro and Howland are both islands in the _____ Ocean.

Ⓐ Atlantic   Ⓑ Pacific   Ⓒ Indian

2 Gerald Gallagher was from _____.

Ⓐ The United States   Ⓑ Britain   Ⓒ The Gilbert Islands

3 The *Norwich City* was a _____.

Ⓐ ship   Ⓑ type of crab   Ⓒ team of people

4 On Nikumaroro, there are many _____.

Ⓐ elephants   Ⓑ airplanes   Ⓒ turtles

5 Nobody saw Amelia after _____.

Ⓐ 1937   Ⓑ 1940   Ⓒ 1991

My Opinion

What happened to Amelia and Fred? Why do you think that? What are your reasons?

What happened:

_____

_____

_____

_____

My reasons:

1 _____

_____

_____

2 _____

_____

_____

3 _____

_____

_____

Answer Key

Words to Know, page 4

❶ gas **❷** take off **❸** ocean **❹** land **❺** island **❻** ship

Words to Know, page 5

❶ flight **❷** hurt **❸** bone **❹** fall **❺** dead

Video Quest, page 5

Because she's a woman who's famous. Because she flew across the Atlantic. Because she's going to fly around the world.

Analyze, page 11

People can use shells, cups, cans, bags, hats . . .

Video Quest, page 15

Betty heard Amelia. She said, "This is Amelia Earhart." She also said, "New York City" or maybe "*Norwich City.*"

Video Quest, page 17

The doctor wanted to see how far crabs can carry bones.

Evaluate, page 19

Answers will vary.

True or False?, page 22

❶ B **❷** A **❸** B **❹** A **❺** B **❻** A **❼** A **❽** B

Choose the Correct Answers, page 23

❶ B **❷** B **❸** A **❹** C **❺** A

My Opinion, page 23

Answers will vary.